Hon A. Felch
Ann Arbor.
Michigan

[From the New Englander, for July, 1873.]

JOEL BARLOW.

By Rev. A. C. BALDWIN, Hartford, Conn.

[From the New Englander, for July, 1873.

JOEL BARLOW.

By Rev. A. C. BALDWIN, Hartford, Conn.

Joel Barlow was one of the celebrities of the latter part of the last century. The present generation know but little about him. The reason is two-fold; first, there is a tendency in mankind to forget those who have gone before them, however great and honorable they may have been, and to suffer their names to pass into obscurity; and secondly, there has been an unwarrantable neglect, on the part of his countrymen, to write his biography. Barlow was not a genius in the highest sense of that term, but his talents, his writings, his patriotism, and his public services, were of a sufficiently high order to deserve of his country a more extended record than a mere sketch in a cyclopedia, biographical dictionary, or collection of poems. And yet it is upon these chiefly that future generations and historians are to depend for their knowledge of a scholar, poet, philanthropist, and diplomate, of whom America may justly be proud. There are sufficient materials extant, even at the present day, to make an interesting and instructive volume; and it is to be regretted that no competent person has as yet seen fit to use them for this purpose. There are documents in existence which are not only creditable to Barlow, as a man of most generous impulses, and as a patriot of enlarged and sagacious views, but if published, would throw much light upon our national history, especially during the last decade of the eighteenth century, and the first of the present. It is not yet too late to write a worthy memoir of Barlow; but it is not probable it will ever be done. It would be difficult, perhaps impossible, at this late period to awaken in the public mind sufficient interest in a literary or public character who flourished so long ago, to warrant the undertaking.

The design of this Article is to give a brief sketch of the life and prominent characteristics of the poet and patriot, and, especially, to present a curious and most interesting letter from his pen, which it is believed has never before been made public. This letter will be given in the sequel.

Joel Barlow was born in the year 1755, in Reading, Conn., a small agricultural town in Fairfield County. His father was a respectable farmer, in moderate pecuniary circumstances, with a family of ten children to support and educate. Of these, Joel was the youngest. In his early boyhood he gave such unmistakable evidences of more than ordinary talent, that his father determined to give him a liberal education. At a suitable age he commenced fitting for college, but before he had completed his preparatory course he had the misfortune to lose his father by death. He was left with a patrimony barely sufficient to defray the expenses of his education.

In 1774, at the age of 18, he entered Dartmouth College, then in its infancy. After remaining there a short time, he removed his relation to Yale College, where he soon distinguished himself for scholarship, especially in the department of belles-lettres. It was during his academic course that he developed a genius for poetry to such an extent as to attract the special notice of his teachers. The late President Dwight was then a tutor in college, and took a deep interest in his pupil, and a friendship was formed between them which continued till death.

It was while Barlow was in college that the Revolutionary war broke out, and his patriotism was such that during the remainder of his collegiate course he often left the groves of

Academus for the battle-field. His vacations he spent in the army as a volunteer, with his musket to his shoulder, ready to suffer any hardship, perform any service, or brave any danger for his country. He distinguished himself for his heroism, it is said, at the memorable battle of White Plains.

In 1778, he graduated at Yale College with distinguished honor, delivering at commencement a poem, entitled "The Prospect of Peace." This poem was exceedingly popular. It was demanded for the press, and soon published at New Haven. This, and one or two other poetical pieces of his which appeared about the same time, established his reputation as a young man of genius and unusual promise.

On leaving college, Barlow commenced the study of law; but his love for his distressed, bleeding country was so intense as to absorb nearly every other feeling. The army, especially that portion of it which was from New England, had in it largely a religious element. It was composed to a great extent of church-going men, who, like their noble commander-in-chief —Washington—felt their entire dependence for success upon an overruling Providence. Hence there was, in some sections, a great demand for chaplains; and Barlow was earnestly solicited to qualify himself for the office, and enter the army in that capacity. Although he had no special predilection for the ministry as a profession, yet the flame of patriotism burned so intensely in his bosom, he was willing to serve his struggling country in any way that promised to help forward her best interests. His friend Dwight had already set him an example, and gone to the field, and was exerting a most happy influence upon the soldiers. Barlow did not hesitate. He threw aside his law-books, and took up theology, and in six weeks presented himself before an association of Congregational ministers for licensure. He was examined and approved, and with his credentials went immediately to the camp, where as a preacher, adviser, and friend, he endeared himself to both officers and soldiers.

While in the army his poetic talent was turned to good account, for, like Dwight, he often fired the hearts of his companions in arms by composing for them a thrilling patriotic ode, or song, which, when set to music, excited the soldiers to such a pitch of enthusiasm as to cause them to be eager for the battle. During the period of his chaplaincy he continued to cultivate an intimacy with the muses, and besides writing fugitive pieces, he planned, and partly executed, an epic poem of considerable dimensions and reach of thought, entitled "The Vision of Columbus."

In 1781 he took the degree of A.M. at Yale, about which time he married a Miss Baldwin of New Haven, to whom we shall again refer.

At the close of the war, Barlow retired both from the army and the ministry. To spend his life as a parish clergyman had never entered into his plans. The clerical profession, as such, was not in accordance with his tastes, and he doubted (probably with good reason) his qualifications for its peculiar labors and responsibilities. Accordingly he resumed the study of law at Hartford, and was admitted to the bar in 1785. Very soon after this, he, in connection with Elisha Babcock, Esq., founded a weekly newspaper, entitled "*The Hartford Mercury.*" A large proportion of the editorials were written by Barlow; and his muse contributed not unfrequently to the "poet's corner." The ability with which this paper was conducted gave it a rapid and extensive circulation,—eclipsing, in its literary character especially, nearly all of its contemporaries.

The poetical reputation of Barlow had by this time become so well established, that the General Association of Congregational Ministers of Connecticut applied to him to prepare a book of Psalmody for the use of the churches under their care. Dr. Watts' version of the Psalms had long been in use in this country, and it was so highly and so justly esteemed, that it was to constitute the basis of the new work; but some of Watts' Psalms were inappropriate to our republican institutions, and needed revision to adapt them to the new order of things. Some were deficient in lyrical and poetic merit, and needed to be discarded; some were redundant; and several of the Psalms Watts had omitted entirely. Barlow acceded to the wishes of the General Association, and in 1785 undertook and accomplished the responsible work committed to him, to their satisfaction, and in some particulars far exceeded their expectations. The alterations he made in Watts were, in the main, judicious and happy,—far more so than most of the amendments (falsely so called) made by modern poetasters. Some of Barlow's original versifications of the Psalms omitted by Dr. Watts are of great beauty, particularly that of Ps. CXXXVII. It is said that Watts always designed to versify that beautiful Psalm, but that he never was conscious of a sufficiently high degree of poetic inspiration to enable him to do justice to his theme. Many had attempted it both before the time of Watts, and after; but every effort had proved a failure. Joel Barlow was the first poet to put that touching portion of Hebrew poetry into English verse without essentially degrading it; and his version remains to this day without a rival. To fully appreciate it, it should be read and compared, stanza by stanza, with the original,—not with the original Hebrew text merely, but with our excellent translation.

"THE BABYLONIAN CAPTIVITY.

"Along the banks where Babel's current flows,
Our captive bands in deep despondence strayed;
While Zion's fall in sad remembrance rose,
Her friends, her children, mingled with the dead.

The tuneless harp, that once with joy we strung,
When praise employed, and mirth inspired the lay,
In mournful silence on the willows hung,
And growing grief prolonged the tedious day.

The barbarous tyrants, to increase our woe,
With taunting smiles, a song of Zion claim;
Bid sacred praise in strains melodious flow,
While they blaspheme the great Jehovah's name.

But how in heathen chains, and lands unknown,
Shall Israel's sons a song of Zion raise?
O hapless Salem, God's terrestrial throne,
Thou land of glory, sacred mount of praise,—

If e'er my memory lose thy lovely name,
If my cold heart neglect my kindred race,
Let dire destruction seize this guilty frame;
My hand shall perish, and my voice shall cease.

Yet shall the Lord who hears when Zion calls,
O'ertake her foes with terror and dismay;
His arm avenge her desolated walls,
And raise her children to eternal day."

Dr. Dwight, in his beautiful version of the same Psalm, commencing

"I love thy kingdom, Lord,"

has come nearer to Barlow in point of excellence than any other lyrist; but Dwight takes so great liberties with the text, that his production would be called, more appropriately, a free paraphrase of the Psalm, or rather a Hymn suggested by reading it. And it is certainly one of the finest hymns in the English language.*

---

* As a literary curiosity, we give a version of this Psalm contained in "The Bay Psalm Book," published at Cambridge, 1640,—the first book printed in this country,—prepared by an association of clergymen, the most prominent of whom was John Eliot of Roxbury, the celebrated apostle to the Indians. If the following is a fair specimen of his poetic genius, it may be truly said that it would be easier to read his Indian Bible than to sing his lyrics.

PSALM CXXXVII.

1. The rivers on of Babilon,
   there when wee did sit downe,
   Yea even then wee mourned when
   wee remembered Sion.
2. Our harp wee did hang it amid,
   upon the willow tree,
   Because there they that us away
   led in captivitee
3. Required of us a song, and thus
   ask't mirth us waste who laid,
   "Sing us among a Sion's song,"
   unto us then they said.
4. The Lord's song sing can wee? being
   in strangers land? then let
   loose her skill my right hand, if I
   Jerusalem forget.
5. Let cleave my tongue my pallate on
   if minde thee doe not I,
   if chiefe joyes o'er I prize not more
   Jerusalem my joy.
6. Remember Lord, Edom's sons' word,
   "unto the ground" said they
   "it rase, it rase," when as it was
   Jerusalem her day.
7. Blest shall hee bee that payeth thee
   daughter of Babilon
   who must bee waste, that which thou hast
   rewarded us upon.
8. O happie hee shall surely bee
   that taketh up, that eke
   thy little ones against the stones
   doth into pieces breake.

To the Psalms, Barlow appended a selection of hymns, a number of which were of his own composition.

This book was cordially welcomed by the Congregational churches of Connecticut, and used by them almost exclusively ten or fifteen years, when it gave place to one similar in its general character, prepared by Dr. (then President) Dwight, by request of the same ecclesiastical body. The chief reason for the change was, reports were rife that Barlow, then residing in Paris, had become tinctured with the prevailing French infidel philosophy; and although that did not corrupt his Psalms and Hymns, written many years before, still our conscientious fathers could no longer *sing* them, any more than they could worship in a building of Gothic architecture called a "church," or unite in prayer with a man called a "priest," especially if he had a Prayer-book before him.

An amusing anecdote—supposed to be authentic—is told in relation to Barlow soon after he had completed his book of Psalmody. There was at that time residing in Connecticut, or rather perambulating the State as his fancy moved him, a singular genius, named Arnold,—part simpleton, part wit,—exceedingly shrewd, and remarkable for his ability to extemporize rhymes. He obtained considerable celebrity by exercising his peculiar gift, and was an object of interest wherever he went; for it was always certain there would be some sport when he was present. Barlow had heard of this nondescript poetaster, and had a good deal of curiosity to see him. One day as he was in New Haven, he stepped into a bookstore, and there was Arnold, making amusement, in his way, for quite a circle of gentlemen. The two were immediately introduced to each other as "brother poets." After a few minutes conversation, Barlow requested Arnold to give him an exhibition of his gift in extemporizing poetry. The latter dropped his head for a few seconds, and then looked up into Barlow's face, and repeated the following stanza:—

"You've proved yourself a sinful cre'tur,
You've murder'd Watts, and spilt the meter;
You've tried the word of God to alter,
And for your pains deserve a halter."

None of the gentlemen present enjoyed this sally of wit as much as Barlow.

About this time he disposed of his interest in "*The Mercury*" to his partner, Mr. Babcock, and devoted a considerable portion of his time to completing and preparing for the press his great epic poem which he projected and commenced when in the army—"The Vision of Columbus"—afterward expanded into "The Columbiad." It was published with flattering success in 1787, and in a few months was reprinted both in London and in Paris. To dispose of his Poem and book of Psalmody, in both of which works he had a considerable pecuniary interest, Barlow opened a bookstore in Hartford. Having accomplished his object, he relinquished his store, and returned to his law studies, which, since his admission to the bar, had received but little of his attention. But the legal profession had no more charms for him than the clerical, and he did not succeed in it. His elocution was somewhat embarrassed, and his manners were not sufficiently familiar and conciliating to make him popular as a lawyer, and win him clients; but more than all, his heart was not in his profession. He was interested in the law as a study, and made respectable proficiency in it, and the attainments he made in legal science were of essential service to him in subsequent life; but the petty, every-day details and frequent vexations of a lawyer's office were disgusting to him; and as an advocate, he knew he could never do himself justice. Literature, on the other hand, was congenial to his taste. Here he was at home, and he enjoyed himself far better in a literary club in Hartford, of which he was a prominent member, than he did in attending the courts. The club alluded to, although formed nearly a century ago, has an honorable record, and is known and spoken of to this day as the "Club of Hartford Wits," consisting originally of Lemuel Hopkins, Joel Barlow, John Trumbull (the author of McFingal), and David Humphreys. It was afterward enlarged by the addition of Richard Alsop, Theodore Dwight, and others. It embodied talent, humor, poetical genius, and political acumen; and its influence was felt not only throughout Connecticut, but in other States. It was a "masked battery" with guns pointing in all directions, and they were well served, as many a writhing victim could testify. This club published a sprightly, caustic, political paper, in verse, called "*The Anarchiad.*" It appeared anonymously in numbers at irregular intervals, and was filled to overflowing with wit, satire, sarcasm, ridicule, and good sense. Its shafts were aimed at the political errors and extravagances of the times. It was during the Confederacy, and just before the formation of our Constitution, when our public affairs were in a very unsatisfactory and chaotic state; and in some places the condition of things bordered on anarchy. The poetical essays issued in concert by these wits in the "*Anarchiad,*" from time to time, purported to be papers excavated from Western ruins, or mounds, recently opened. Their true origin, however, was pretty well understood, and their effect upon the public mind was most happy in arresting the rapid progress of misrule among the masses, and tendency to rebellion, which had already broken out under the leadership of Shays in Massachusetts. Barlow was a large contributor to the "*Anarchiad,*" and wrote some of its best numbers.

By this time our poet was getting into somewhat straitened pecuniary circumstances. His small patrimony had been expended in his education; his law business would hardly pay his office rent; the profits on his Psalm-book and Vision of Columbus were not large, and the money received from those sources was nearly or quite exhausted. His contributions to the *Anarchiad*, and other political papers, were unremunerative, and his connection with the "Club" was productive of more amusement than cash. He had a prudent and amiable wife, but prudence and amiability on her part could not pay house rent, nor furnish the larder and wardrobe. Starvation began to stare Barlow in the face, and he saw that at this rate he would inevitably, and very soon, be put upon "short allowance." Something must be done. Just at this crisis, one of those dashing, brilliant humbugs, which about once in twenty years have from time immemorial bedazzled and duped the public with promises of large and sudden wealth to all its patrons, was brought out from its infernal den, where such things are concocted by the knowing ones, and attracted almost universal attention. It was a great "Land Company," which had come in possession (it was claimed, and generally believed) of immense tracts of land of great value, chiefly in the

State of Ohio. These lands the Company were anxious to sell, and proposed terms which were *sure to make the purchaser rich in a very short time.* The bait took, of course. As there was but very little capital in the country at that time which could be spared for investment, the Company hoped to effect large sales in Europe. As Barlow was in want of remunerative employment, he accepted an agency to dispose of these lands in foreign countries, and in 1788 embarked for England with sanguine hopes of success. He remained in England only a short time, when he crossed over to France; the latter country appearing to him a more promising field for operations. Here he succeeded in disposing of some of the lands claimed by his employers. But just as success was beginning to crown his efforts, *the bubble burst.* It was ascertained that this famous "Scioto Land Company," as it was called, was nothing more nor less than a gigantic band of swindling speculators; that they were selling lands to which they had no better title than that arch land-speculator of old had to "the kingdoms of the world," which he offered to dispose of for a trifling consideration. Whatever pretended titles this Company had to the lands in question, it was proved that they had been procured by a series of fraudulent transactions, which of course rendered them good for nothing. Barlow embarked in this enterprise in good faith, not having the least suspicion that he was linking himself with an association of knaves and sharpers; but as soon as he was made acquainted with the true character of the concern, in anger, mortification, and disgust, he threw up his agency, from which he had received very little pecuniary benefit.

The circumstances in which Barlow now found himself were peculiarly trying. He was in a foreign land, without money, without employment, without influential friends on whom he could rely for aid, and dependent entirely on his mental resources for the support of himself and wife. His old friends and associates in America felt considerable solicitude for him, being uncertain what were his condition and prospects. Trumbull, in a letter to Oliver Wolcott, Dec. 9th, 1789, says; "I cannot conceive what Barlow is doing. After being eighteen months abroad, you tell me 'he has got so far as to see favorable prospects. If he should not effect something soon, I would advise him to write *The Visions of Barlow*, as a sequel to those of Columbus and McFingal."

For the following three or four years, Barlow relied chiefly upon the products of his pen for subsistence. Part of the time he resided in France, and part of the time in England. In both countries he acquired quite a reputation as a writer, and his influence began to be extensively felt. Being at heart a sincere and earnest Republican, he took a deep interest in the cause of freedom for which he had fought and labored so hard and so persistently at home. France was then in the midst of her great Revolution, and divided into diverse contending factions. The sympathies of Barlow were wholly with the "Girondists," or moderate Republicans, who took a decided stand against the "Jacobins" on the one side, and irrepressible Monarchists on the other. To this party he gave his aid and influence, so far as his position as a foreigner would permit him, and he gained with it a high degree of popularity.

When in England, Barlow published several poems of a political character, which produced quite a sensation in high places, and which brought the author conspicuously before the British public. One of these was entitled "Advice to the Privileged Orders;" and another was "The Conspiracy of Kings." Both of these were productions of great vigor and point. Although France was professedly the object aimed at, yet England was constantly kept in view. In fact these poems were both of them sharp swords with two edges, and Barlow designed to have them cut both ways; and they did. The first was an attack upon the feudal Aristocracies of Europe, as they were related to the Church, the Army, the Judiciary, the Revenue, and Public Expenditure; and it was so skillfully done, that it elicited from Fox a formal eulogy in the House of Commons. The second was an *exposé*, for public reprobation, of the first coalition of crowned heads against France.

In September, 1792, Barlow took the liberty to address a letter, on his own responsibility, to the French "National Convention," making some important suggestions in regard to their Constitution; reccommending a separation of Church and State, and some other important reforms. Soon after this, the "London Constitutional Society," a body of reformers in England, voted an address to the "Convention" at Paris, and deputed Barlow, who was a member of their body, to pass over to France, and present it in person. He was received with great cordiality, and the Convention, in token of their respect for him personally, conferred on him the honor and the rights of French citizenship.

The prominent interest Barlow took in Constitutional Republicanism, and especially the compliment paid him by the Convention at Paris, awakened the jealousies, or rather increased and intensified those already existing, of the British aristocracy toward him; and he was suspected (unjustly) of being engaged in a secret plot to revolutionize the government. His mission to France, they said, "must have some covert design," and the matter was officially investigated, and although nothing was discovered which implicated Barlow as plotting against England, more than against injustice and oppression every where, still it was not deemed, by his friends, prudent for him to return thither. He therefore determined to make Paris his residence, and sent to England for Mrs. Barlow.

Soon after this, he accompanied a deputation of the Convention to Savoy, for the purpose of organizing that territory as a department of the French Republic, although he did not go in an official capacity. The deputation, however, sought his counsel, and paid much deference to his opinions.

While at Chamberry, the capital of Savoy, at the request of friends, he addressed a letter to the inhabitants of Piedmont, setting forth the advantages of a republic, inciting them to throw off their allegiance to the "Man of Turin, who called himself their king," and follow the example of their French neighbors. This address was translated into the French and Italian languages, and widely circulated.

While at this place, he wrote also the most amusing and, perhaps, upon the whole, the most popular poem he ever composed, "Hasty-pudding," a mock heroic in three cantos, which no genuine Yankee ever read or can read without interest. In it our author gives a minute history of *a bowl of hasty-pudding and milk*, in all the processes of preparing the ground, planting, cultivating, gathering, and grinding the corn,—not omitting the sports of rustic swains and nymphs at husking-time, — the housewife's transmutation of the golden meal into the delicious pudding, the care and milking of the cow, in short, every thing and every process pertaining to the subject, till the consumption of the rich repast from

"The wide-mouthed bowl, safe poised upon the knee."

In the whole poem, there is such a commingling of stately, grandiloquent diction, and ludicrous, rustic simplicity, as constitutes the soul of wit, and the attention of the reader is enchained from the beginning to the end.

Our author prefaces his poem by a very sensible letter to Mrs. George Washington, recommending the higher classes of society to practice simplicity of diet, not only because it is a virtue in itself, but especially on account of the influence their example would exert upon the common people.

From Savoy, Barlow returned to Paris, where he resided about three years. His interest in the political renovation of France was unabated; but the excesses, the extravagances, the fanaticism, and at length, the injustice and horrible atrocities of many in power who called themselves Reformers, were such as to shock the feelings of an enlightened philanthropist like Barlow, and his faith was much shaken in regard to the ultimate beneficent results of the Revolution. Consequently from this time he stood aloof almost entirely from French politics, and gave his attention to business.

Politicians were exceedingly anxious to avail themselves of his well known popularity in Paris, and occasionally violent political Articles would appear in the papers purporting to have been written by him; but they were soon ascertained to be forgeries. His position in France as a neutral, enjoying as he did the privileges which had been conferred on him of citizenship, gave him frequent opportunities of engaging in profitable commercial transactions, of which he availed himself; and he soon rose above all pecuniary embarrassment, or even any solicitude in that direction. His literary labors were for a while nearly suspended, with the exception of preparing a translation of "Volney's Ruins."

In 1795, Barlow was employed as an agent for the transaction of important legal and commercial business, of a private nature, in the north of Europe. On his return, he found awaiting him a commission from America, appointing him United States Consul for Algiers, with power to negotiate a treaty with the Dey; and also with instructions to redeem all Americans held in slavery on the Barbary coast. Many of our citizens were at that time suffering extreme hardships in those piratical, lawless States, having been captured at sea by freebooters, or shipwrecked upon their inhospitable shores, and were held as slaves, or captives, until large sums should be paid for their ransom.

Barlow accepted the commission, and immediately entered upon the important and difficult undertaking. In many respects it was a *dangerous* one. He had to deal with ignorant, half-civilized, unprincipled men. The climate where he was going was sickly in the extreme, and that most terrible scourge of the human race—the plague—was then raging with fearful mortality in the city of Algiers. But Barlow did not hesitate. He was not influenced in the least by pecuniary considerations. He was accumulating property in Paris very rapidly, and had already amassed a respectable fortune. The office to which he was appointed was no sinecure; on the contrary, the acceptance of it involved, on his part, a great pecuniary sacrifice. But he made it, and he made it cheerfully. With a patriotism, and in the exercise of a philanthropy worthy of all praise, but never duly appreciated, he gave himself to the work entrusted to him by Washington.

Barlow was so deeply impressed with the perils of his undertaking, that he hardly expected to survive. Accordingly, he "put his house in order," made his will anew, and settled all his worldly affairs as if he knew that he should never return.

Having made every provision possible for the comfort and happiness of Mrs. Barlow during his absence,—for to take her with him was out of the question,—he took leave of her, and passing through Spain, and across the Mediterranean, he hastened to Algiers. When he reached the city, he immediately set himself about negotiating a treaty with the Dey. In this he was much embarrassed by the opposition and intrigues of several European agents; but with much shrewdness and tact, he thwarted their machinations, and concluded the treaty expeditiously. He soon after negotiated a similiar treaty with Tripoli, and another with Tunis. But the great object constantly before Barlow's mind was *the liberation of his distressed countrymen from their pitiable condition as slaves, or prisoners, and preparing for them the means to return to their homes.* To secure these desirable ends, he spared himself no labor ; he was intimidated by no hostility ; he was discouraged by no obstacles ; he shrank from no personal danger. His life was in constant peril. Like Paul, he was literally "in journeyings often, in perils of waters, in perils of robbers, in perils by the heathen, in perils in the city, in perils in the wilderness, in perils in the sea ; in weariness and painfulness, in watchings often, in hunger and thirst." In a letter to his wife [see the close of this Article], dated Algiers, 8th July, 1796, he says : "The plague is raging with considerable violence in this place, and I must tell you that a pressing duty of humanity requires me to expose myself more than other considerations would justify, in endeavoring to save as many of our unhappy citizens as possible from falling a sacrifice, and embark them, at this cruel moment, for their country."

Barlow's mission was eminently successful, as it might be supposed it would be, undertaken with so much self denial, and prosecuted with such untiring zeal, energy, and perseverance. In the course of two years, he negotiated three important treaties, in spite of the most formidable and discouraging obstacles, and ransomed all the American capitives held by the Barbary powers who could be found.

Having accomplished the main object for which he undertook the duties and assumed the responsibilities of the Consulate, he resigned his commission in 1797, and returned to Paris. He here led a private life for several years, engaged for the most part in commercial transactions, some of which proved very advantageous, so that his fortune,—ample before,—was much increased ; and he purchased and occupied one of the splendid residences of the city, to which with the largest hospitality, he ever bade his countrymen a cordial welcome.

About this time, serious difficulties arose between the United States and France, growing out of the interference of the latter country with our commerce. Barlow watched the progress of affairs with great solicitude, being friendly to both parties ; he used all his influence to bring about a good understanding between them. He took an impartial view of the case, and addressed letters to each of the two Governments, criticizing what he believed to have been wrong, and giving with great force of language his views of maritime law and the rights of neutrals,—points on which the two nations did not harmonize.

In 1805, Barlow returned with his wife to his native land, after an absence of seventeen years. He went from home poor, an agent of what proved to be a swindling land company: he returned in possession of large wealth, honorably acquired; with new literary laurels on his brow, and with a high reputation as a politician, diplomate, and philanthropist, both in the old world and the new.

Soon after his return, he purchased a beautiful situation in Washington, near Georgetown, on which he erected a fine mansion, and laid out the ample grounds with exquisite taste, adorning them with trees, shrubs, and flowers, so that "Kalorama," as he named the establishment, became for those days one of the most delightful spots in America. Here he lived in elegant retirement, his hospitable doors always open, enjoying the friendship of the President and most of the leading men of the nation, and the respect of all.

But Barlow was not the man to rust in idleness because he had become rich, and could afford to do so. One of his first efforts, after his return, was to secure, if possible, the establishment of a National University under the patronage of the Government, which should combine a college—a learned society somewhat after the French model—a school of the fine arts, and a military and naval academy. He prepared circulars, showing the advantages to the country of such an institution, and at his own expense had them printed and scattered broadcast all over the United States. At one time there was a fair prospect of success, but finally the project fell through for want of Congressional coöperation. A bill for the establishment of such a university was introduced in the Senate, and met with favor, and was referred to a special committee; but that committee have not reported to this day.

Disappointed in his favorite project, Barlow gave special attention to his literary studies, which he had never wholly suspended. He recast the epic poem of his early days—"The

Visions of Columbus"—which after many additions and amendments he republished in 1808, with the title "The Columbiad." This was a poem of striking excellencies, and prominent defects. The literary world were much divided in their opinion of its merits. Some of the critics were extravagant in their praises; others as much so in their censure. Its intrinsic merit, considered æsthetically, lay about midway between these extremes. The conception of the poem was certainly a grand one. The plan of it is thus concisely and beautifully given by the Rev. C. W. Everest, the compiler of an interesting volume, "The Poets of Connecticut."

"The Columbiad consists of a series of visions presented by Hesper, the guardian Genius of the Western continent to Columbus, while languishing in the prison of Valladolid, where he is first introduced awaking from a painful, delirious sleep, and uttering a mournful monologue upon his ill-requited services. The hero and his Genius quit the dungeon, and ascend the mount of vision which rises over the western coast of Spain. Europe settles from their sight; the Atlantic is spread beneath their feet, and the continent of America is revealed to their view. The visions then exhibit successively, in the order of time, the conquest and settlement of South America—the settlement, by various colonies, of North America—the most brilliant exploits of the Revolutionary war—the Federal system of America, and the universal benefit which should attend

'The well-based brotherhood, the league divine.'

The scene then embraces the whole earth, displays the future progress and improvements of society in all the arts and sciences, and as a last view exhibits a general congress from all nations, amicably assembled to establish the political harmony of all mankind. The Genius thus cheers the heart of the daring voyager at the close:

'Here, then,' said Hesper with a blissful smile,
'Behold the fruits of thy long years of toil.
To yon bright borders of Atlantic day,
Thy swelling pinions led the trackless way,
And taught mankind such useful deeds to dare,
To trace new seas, and happy nations rear,
Till by fraternal hands their sails unfurled
Have waved at last in union o'er the world.
Then let thy steadfast soul no more complain
Of dangers braved and griefs endured in vain,
Of courts insidious, envy's poisoned stings,
The loss of empire and the frown of kings;
While these broad views thy better thoughts compose
To spurn the malice of insulting foes;
And all the joys descending ages gain,
Repay thy labors and remove thy pain.'

It may safely be affirmed that there is more genuine poetry in the bare *conception* of the Columbiad than is to be found in *all the works* of many pretentious bards of considerable note; and our author may well be pardoned for some imperfections in the execution of his plan.

The Columbiad was first issued in a style of elegance surpassing that of any book previously published in this country, and dedicated to his life-long friend, Robert Fulton, who, at his own expense, illustrated it by numerous plates executed by the best artists in Europe. Its price was consequently so high as to place it out of the reach of any but the wealthy; but it was followed, not long after, by a cheaper edition. It was soon republished in England, where it received a severe handling, of course.

After issuing the Columbiad, Barlow contemplated publishing a history of the United States. While engaged in collecting and arranging materials for such a work, he, in 1811, received from our Government the appointment of Minister Plenipotentiary to the court of France. Several complicated and difficult questions were to be settled with that nation, the chief of which was the old one of "French spoliations," and we have not heard the last of it yet. There was no man in America so competent to manage these matters as Barlow, and he was induced to accept the mission.

On his arrival in France, his first effort was to negotiate a treaty of commerce for the future, and to obtain indemnity for the past; but he was thwarted at every step by the opposition and strategies of French diplomates. Barlow was faithful and persistent, and was determined not to be out-generaled by any of them, and if his life had been spared it is probable that success would have crowned his efforts sooner or later. Bonaparte's famous "Berlin and Milan decrees" had been a source of great annoyance and injustice to America. By the latter of these decrees, every neutral vessel which submitted to British search, or consented to any pecuniary exactions whatever, was to be seized and confiscated. Barlow wished very much to have a personal interview with the Emperor to discuss these and kindred topics. In October, 1812, when Napoleon was invading Russia, he was invited, much to his joy, to a conference with the Emperor, at Wilna, in Poland. He started immediately on his mission, and traveled with all possible expedition, day and night, lest he should lose some advantage by delay. His route led him through a section of country just desolated by war to such an extent that it was almost impossible to obtain a comfortable and wholesome meal. The weather, as he advanced northward, became unusually severe. The only places of entertainment were small Jewish cottages, densely crowded, and heated up to a high temperature, according to the custom of the Polanders. The frequent alternations of extreme heat and cold, want of sleep, and proper food, combined with great fatigue and exhaustion, were too much for his constitution, robust as it was. They produced a violent inflammation of the lungs, from which he did not recover. He rapidly sank into a state of extreme debility and torpor, which resulted in death, December 22, 1812, at Zarnawica, an obscure village in Poland, near Cracow.

The death of Barlow created quite a sensation, both in this country and in Europe. He was, to say the least, one of the ablest, most patriotic, and unselfish men that had ever represented America in the Old World; and few, if any, had contributed more largely than he to secure for his native land the respect of other nations. France, especially, was moved by the intelligence of his decease. In Paris, honors were paid to his memory far beyond those usually paid to foreigners of distinction. A glowing epitaph of him was composed by one of the most celebrated French writers, and an appreciative eulogy was pronounced before one of her prominent national societies, by Dupont de Nemours, representing him as a man of letters, and as a wise, patriotic, and faithful public functionary. Extracts from the Columbiad, translated into French heroic verse, were soon afterward published in Paris, in connection with a sketch of his life, character, and writings.

In private life, Mr. Barlow was much respected and beloved. He had an amiable disposition and took much pleasure in contributing to the happiness of all around him. His manners were somewhat grave and dignified. In conversation, he was not remarkably fluent or sprightly, especially in mixed company, where he was often reserved and absent-minded. When with his intimate friends, however, or when excited by some interesting topic, he would converse with great animation, frequently throwing off brilliant scintillations of wit and humor.

In his domestic relations, Mr. Barlow was preëminently happy. Soon after his graduation he was united in marriage with Miss Ruth Baldwin, daughter of Michael Baldwin, Esq., of New Haven, a native of North Guilford, Conn. She had two brothers distinguished in public life,—Hon. Abraham Baldwin, who soon after resigning his tutorship in Yale College, removed to Georgia, and is well known in history as President of her University,—one of her delegates to the convention that formed the original Constitution of the United States, and subsequently a senator in Congress from that State till his death. He was never married. The other brother was the late Hon. Henry Baldwin, of Pittsburgh, Pa., one of the judges of the United States Supreme Court.

Miss Baldwin was a lady of superior intellect, amiable disposition, dignified, yet easy and graceful in her manners, and of unusual personal attractions. These characteristics she retained until death, which occurred May 30, 1818. The writer of this Article remembers distinctly—although a lad at the time—her interesting conversation and graceful bearing when, past the age of sixty, she spent a night at his father's house.

The affection of Mr. Barlow for his lovely wife was unusually strong, and on her part it was fully reciprocated. She cheerfully, in early life, cast in her lot with his "for better or for worse;"—and sometimes the *worse*, so far as their pecuniary prospects were concerned, seemed to be in the ascendant. In their darkest days—and some of them were very dark—Barlow ever found light and encouragement at home in the smiles, sympathy, and counsel of his prudent, faithful wife. No matter how black and portentous the cloud that brooded over them might be, she always contrived to give it a "silver lining," and his subsequent success in life he always attributed more to her influence over him than to any thing else. Hence, the reader will be enabled to appreciate those terms and expressions of endearment in a letter of his to her which supplements this Article,—terms and expressions which might to some appear extravagant, not to say silly, if used by a young Benedict during the raptures of the "honey-moon," but which do honor to the heart of a husband after many years of married life.

The letter to which we allude is a curiosity in its way, full of affection, confidence, benevolence, sound judgment, and common sense. As Mr. and Mrs. Barlow had no children, he bestowed upon her, for life, all his property, untrammelled by those ungenerous and contemptible conditions which so often are attached to such bequests, even when there has been the most perfect fidelity, harmony, and affection on both sides. Jealousy in any circumstance, is a most unlovely passion, but it never appears more so than when exercised toward an imaginary possible successor in the affections of a devoted, loving companion. Barlow, in his letter, demonstrated how utterly void his heart was of any such unworthy, unmanly feeling; and the most remarkable and curious part of the epistle is his apostrophe to such a hypothetical successor.

We know our readers will be gratified to peruse entire this unique production, and will thank us for giving them an opportunity to do so. It was written, it should be recollected, when Barlow was performing his labors of love in Algiers, during the prevalence of the plague in that city, and when he thought it quite probable he himself might fall a victim to that terrible scourge. But he was mercifully spared. This document was found among his papers after his decease, more than sixteen years from its date.

THE LETTER.

ALGIERS, 8th July, 1796.

TO MRS. BARLOW, IN PARIS:

My dearest Life, and only Love—I run no risk of alarming your extreme sensibility by writing this letter, since it is not my intention that it shall come into your hands unless and until, through some other channel, you shall have been informed of the event which it anticipates as possible. For our happy union to be dissolved by death, is indeed at every moment possible; but at this time, there is an uncommon degree of danger that you may lose a life which I know you value more than you do your own. I say I *know* this, because I have long been taught, from our perfect sympathy of affection, to judge your heart by mine; and I can say solemnly and truly, as far as I know myself, that I have no other value for my own life than as a means of continuing a conjugal union with the best of women—the wife of my soul—my first, my last, my only love.

I have told you, in my current letters, that the plague is raging with considerable violence in this place. I must tell you in this, if it should be your fortune to see it, that a pressing duty of humanity requires me to expose myself more than other considerations would justify, in endeavoring to save as many of our unhappy citizens as possible from falling a sacrifice, and to embark them at this cruel moment for their country.

Though they are dying very fast, yet it is possible my exertions may be the means of saving a number who otherwise would perish. If this should be the case, and *I* should fall instead of *them*, my tender, generous friend must not upbraid my memory by ever *thinking* I did too much. But she cannot help it—I know she cannot. Yet, my dearest love, give me leave, since I must anticipate your affliction, to lay before you some reflections, which would occur to you at *last*, but which ought to strike your mind at *first*, to mingle with, and assuage your first emotions of grief.

You cannot judge at your distance of the risque I am taking, nor of the necessity of taking it; and I am convinced that, were you in my place, you would do more than I shall do; for your kind, intrepid spirit has more courage than mine, and always had.

Another consideration;—many of these persons have wives at home as well as I, from whom they have been much longer separated, under more affecting circumstances,—having been held in a merciless and desponding slavery. If their wives love them as mine does me (a thing I cannot believe, but have no right to deny), ask these lately disconsolate, and now joyous, families whether I have done too much?

Since I write this as if it were the last poor demonstration of my affection to my lovely friend, I have much to say; and it is with difficulty that I can steal an hour from the fatigue of business to devote to the grateful, painful task. But tell me (you cannot tell me), where shall I begin? where shall I end? how shall I put an eternal period to a correspondence which has given me so much comfort? with what expression of regret shall I take leave of my happiness? with what words of tenderness, of gratitude, of counsel, of consolation, shall I pay you for what I am robbing you of,—the husband whom you cherish,—the friend who is all your own?

But I am giving vent to more weakness than I intended. This, my dear, is a letter of *business*, not of love, and I wonder I cannot enter upon it, and keep to my subject.

Enclosed is my last Will, made in conformity to the one I left in the hands of Dr. Hopkins of Hartford, as you may remember. The greater part of our property now lying in Paris, I thought proper to renew this instrument, that you might enter immediately upon the settlement of your affairs, without waiting to send to America for the other paper.

You will likewise find enclosed a schedule of our property, debts, and demands, with explanations, as nearly just as I can make it from memory in the absence of my papers. If the French Republic is consolidated and her funds rise to par, or near it, as I believe they will do soon after the war, the effects noted in this schedule may amount to a capital of about $120,000, besides paying my debts;—which sum vested in the American funds, or mortgages equally solid, would produce something more than $7,000 a year perpetual income.

If the French should fund their debt anew at one half its nominal value (which is possible), so that the part of your property now vested in those funds should diminish in proportion, still, taking the whole together, it will not make a difference of more than one-third; and the annual income may still be near $5,000. Events unforseen by me may, however, reduce it considerably lower. But whatever the value may be of what I leave, it is bequeathed simply and wholly to you.

Perhaps some of my relations may think it strange that I have not mentioned them in this final disposition of my effects, especially if they should prove to be as considerable as I hope they may. But, my dearest love, I will tell you my reasons, and I hope you will approve them. For if I can excuse myself to *you* in a point in which your generous delicacy would be more likely to question the propriety of my conduct than in most others, I am sure my arguments will be convincing to those whose objections may arise from their interest.

First. In a view of justice and equity, whatever we possess at this moment, is a joint property between ourselves, and ought to remain to the survivor. When you gave me your blessed self, you know I was destitute of every other possession, as of every other enjoyment. I was rich only in the fund of your affectionate economy, and the sweet consolation of your society. In our various struggles, and disappointments, while trying to obtain a moderate competency for the quiet enjoyment of what we used to call the remainder of our lives, I have often been rendered happy by misfortunes; for the heaviest we have met with were turned into blessings by the opportunities they gave me to discover new virtues in you, who taught me how to bear them.

I have often told you since the year 1791, the period of our deepest difficulties (and even during that period), that I had never been so easy and contented before. And I have certainly been happier in you during the latter years of our union than I was in the former years;—not that I have loved you more ardently, or more exclusively, for that was impossible; but I have loved you *better;* my heart has been more full of your excellence, and less agitated with objects of ambition, which used to devour me too much.

I recall these things to your mind, to convince you of my full belief, that the acquisition of the competency, which we seem at last to have secured, is owing more to your energy than my own; I mean the energy of your virtues, which gave me consolation, and even happiness, under circumstances wherein, if I had been alone, or with a partner no better than myself, I should have sunk.

These fruits of our joint exertions you expected to enjoy *with me;* else I know you would not have wished for them. But if by my death you are to be deprived of the greater part of the comfort you expected, it would surely be unjust and cruel to deprive you of the remainder, or any portion of it, by giving even a part of this property to others. It is yours in the truest sense in which property can be considered; and I should have no right, if I were disposed, to take it from you.

Secondly. Of *my* relations, I have some thirty or forty nephews and nieces and their children, the greater part of whom I have never seen, and from whom I have had no news for seven or eight years; among them there may be some necessitous ones who would be proper objects of particular legacies, yet it would be impossible for me at this moment to know which they are. It was my intention, and still is, if I live to go to America, to make discriminations among them according to their wants, and to give them such relief as might be in my power, without waiting to do it by legacy. Now, my lovely wife, if this task, and the means of performing it, should devolve on you, I need not recommend it; our *joint* liberality would have been less extensive, and less grateful to the receivers than *yours* will be alone.

Your own relations in the same degrees of affinity are few in number. I hope I need not tell you that in my affections I know no difference between yours and mine. I include them all in the same recommendation, without any other distinction than what may arise from their wants, and your ability to do them good.

If Colonel B******* and his wife (or either of them being left by the other) should be in a situation otherwise than comfortable, I wish my generous friend to render it so, as far as may be in her power. We may have had more powerful friends than they, but never any more sincere. *He* has the most frank and loyal spirit in the world; and *she* is possessed of many amiable and almost heroic virtues.

Mary ********, poor girl! you know her worth, her virtues, and her talents; and I am sure you will not fail to keep yourself informed of her circumstances. She has friends, or at least *had* them, more able than you will be to yield her assistance in case of need. But they may forsake her for reasons which, to your enlightened and benevolent mind, would rather be an additional inducement to contribute to her happiness.

Excuse me, my dearest life, for my being so particular on a subject which, considering to whom it is addressed, may appear superfluous; but I do it rather to show that I agree with you in these sentiments, than to pretend that they originate on my part. With this view, I must pursue them a little farther.

One of the principal gratifications in which I intended, and still intend to indulge myself, if I should live to enjoy with you the means of doing it, is to succor the unfortunate of every description as far as possible,—to encourage merit where I find it,—and try to create it where it does not exist. This has long been a favorite project with me; but having been always destitute of the means of carrying it into effect to any considerable degree, I have not conversed with you upon it as much as I wish I had. Though I can say nothing that will be new to you on the pleasure of employing one's attention and resources in this way, yet some useful hints might be given on the means of multiplying good actions from small resources; for I would not confine my pleasure to the simple duties of *charity*, in the beggar's sense of the word.

First. Much may be done by advising with poor persons,—contriving for them,—and pointing out the objects on which they can employ their own industry.

Secondly. Many persons and families, in a crisis of difficulty, might be extricated, and set up in the world, by little loans of money for which they might give good security, and refund within a year; and the same fund might then go to relieve a second, and a third; and thus a dozen families might be set on the independent footing of their own industry, in the course of a dozen years, by the help of fifty dollars, and the owner lose nothing but the interest. Some judgment would be necessary in these operations, as well as care and attention, in finding out the proper objects. How many of these are to be found in prisons,—thrown in and confined for years, for small debts, which their industry and their liberty would enable them to discharge in a short time!

Imprisonment for debt still exists as a stain upon our country, as most others. France indeed has set us the example of abolishing it; but I am apprehensive she will relapse from this, as I see she is inclined to do from many other good things which she began in her magnanimous struggle for the renovation of society.

Thirdly. With your benevolence, your character, and connections, you may put in motion a much greater fund of charity than you will yourself possess. It is by searching out the objects of distress, or misfortune, and recommending them to their wealthy neighbors in such a manner as to excite their attention. I have often remarked to you (I forget whether you agree with me in it or not) that there is more goodness at the bottom of the human heart than the world will generally allow. Men are as often hindered from doing a generous thing by an *indolence*, either of thought or action, as by a selfish principle. If they knew what the action was, when and where it was to be done, and how to do it, their obstacles would be overcome. In this manner one may bring the resources of others into contribution, and with such a grace as to obtain the thanks both of the givers and receivers.

Fourthly. The *example* of one beneficent person, like yourself, in a neighborhood or a town, would go a great way. It would doubtless be imitated by others, extend far, and benefit thousands whom you might never hear of.

I certainly hope to escape from this place, and return to your beloved arms. No man has stronger inducements to wish to live than I have. I have no quarrel with the world; it has used me as well as could be expected. I have valuable friends in every country where I have put my foot, not excepting this abominable sink of wickedness, pestilence, and folly,—the city of Algiers. I have a pretty extensive and dear-bought knowledge of mankind; a most valuable collection of books; a pure and undivided taste for domestic tranquility; the social intercourse of friends; study; and the exercise of charity. I have a moderate but sufficient income; perfect health; an unimpaired constitution; and to give the relish to all enjoyments, and smooth away the asperities that might arise from unforseen calamities, I have the wife that my youth chose, and my advancing age has cherished,—the pattern of excellence,—the example of every virtue,—from whom all my joys have risen, in whom all my hopes are centered.

I will use every precaution for my safety, as well for your sake as mine. But if you should see me no more, my dearest friend, you will not forget I loved you. As you have valued my love, and as you believe this letter is written with an intention to promote your happiness at a time when it will be forever out of my power to contribute to it in any other way, I beg you will kindly receive the last advice I can give you, with which I am going to close our endearing intercourse. * * * * * * * * * * * Submitting with patience to a destiny that is unavoidable, let your tenderness for me soon cease to agitate that lovely bosom; banish it to the house of darkness and dust, with the object that can no longer be benefited by it, and transfer your affections to some worthy person who shall supply my place in the relation I have borne to you. It is for the living, not the dead, to be rendered happy by the sweetness of your temper, the purity of your heart, your exalted sentiments, your cultivated spirit, your undivided love. Happy man of your choice! should he know and prize the treasure of such a wife! O treat her tenderly, my dear sir; she is used to nothing but kindness, unbounded love and confidence. She is all that any reasonable man can desire. She is more than I have merited, or perhaps than you can merit. My resigning her to your charge, though but the result of uncontrolable necessity, is done with a degree of cheerfulness,—a cheerfulness inspired by the hope that her happiness will be the object of your care, and the long-continued fruit of your affection.

Farewell, my wife; and though I am not used to subscribe my letters addressed to you, your familiarity with my writing having always rendered it unnecessary, yet it seems proper that the last characters which this hand shall trace for your perusal should compose the name of your most faithful, most affectionate, and most grateful husband, JOEL BARLOW.

www.ingramcontent.com/pod-product-compliance
Lightning Source LLC
LaVergne TN
LVHW011141110826
845150LV00008B/2448
* 9 7 8 1 4 1 8 1 9 3 0 4 1 *